Esteem-Builders
for
Children's Ministry

Edited by Beth Rowland

Group
Loveland, Colorado

Contributors

Judi Bailey
Carolyn Beyer
Judy Brown
Nanette Goings
Sheila Halasz
Lyn Jackson
Ellen Javernick
Janel Kauffman
Corinne Bergstrom Linker

Brian Mason
Cindy Newell
Lori Haynes Niles
Authorene Phillips
Vicki Shannon
Linda Shepherd
Betty Stilwell
Terry Vermillion
Peggy Whitt

Esteem-Builders for Children's Ministry
Copyright © 1992 Group Publishing, Inc.

First Printing

Credits
Edited by Beth Rowland
Cover designed by Bob Fuller
Interior designed by Dori Walker
Illustrations by Anita Dufalla

Scripture quoted from The Youth Bible, New Century Version, copyright © 1991 by Word Publishing, Dallas, Texas 75039. Used by permission.

Library of Congress Cataloging-in-Publication Data

ISBN 1-55945-174-2
Printed in the United States of America

CONTENTS

Introduction 12

Building Esteem From Teacher to Child

Willy Worm 16
Cheer up children when they've been disappointed.

Just Because..16
Show children you care about them just because.

The Kindness Worm 17
Children charm a worm puppet out of a basket with their kind actions.

Animal Goodbyes 17
Send children home with goodbyes from their favorite animals.

I Love You in Lots of Languages 18
Say, "I love you" in a variety of languages.

You're Great! 18
Try these ideas to tell children they've done a super job.

Encouraging Words..19
Show children their efforts don't go unnoticed.

Spare Hugs..19
Ask kids for spare hugs and tell them you and Jesus love them.

Growing 19
Let children know you've noticed their actions.

The Very Important People Book..20
Make a class scrapbook.

Keep in Touch..21
Show children you are interested in them and their activities.

Take a Little Time 21
    Visit children to let them know they're special.

Missing Children...21
    Send cards to tell children you care.

Candid Camera...22
    Notice children's efforts to be Christlike.

There's a Flower in You...22
Recognize the positive traits children have and their potential for growth.

I'm Thinking 23
    Play a guessing game using children's good traits.

Golden Apple Delight 24
    Notice children's kind words and tell them you appreciate them.

Caring Cats 26
    Show kids you've seen them caring for one another.

We Miss You When You're Gone...28
    Show children how important they are to the class.

Decisions, Decisions..29
    Ask for children's help with class decisions.

Spotlights 29
    Give each child the chance to stand in the spotlight.

Interview the Flock..30
    Spend individual time getting to know each child.

Whose Birthday Is It, Anyway? 31
    On your birthday, thank the children for their friendship.

Half Birthdays 31
    Remember children on their half birthdays.

Cookie Kisses..31
        Individually affirm your children with cookie kisses.

The Barnabas Connection 32
        Hand out secret awards that tell children
        you've seen them encourage one another.

Mirror Writing 33
        Write secret messages that tell children they're special.

Building Esteem From God to Child

One Lost Sheep..36
        Show children that God loves them as much as the shepherd
                who hunted for one lost sheep.

Guess Who God Loves...38
                Show children that they are loved by God.

Jesus Loves You 38
        Remind children of Jesus' love with a game variation that's lively and fun.

This Is Our Class 39
                Use a video to celebrate.

The Seal of the King 40
        Make reminders of the special promises God makes to his people.

Sweet-Smelling Acts 41
        Teach children that God thinks they're a beautiful fragrance.

God Loves Me Go-Around..41
        Children come up with qualities that God loves about them.

Rainbows 42
        Teach children that God remembers each of them.

Reflecting God's Light..43
Show children that God wants them to shine for him.

A Gift From God 43
Kids tell one another that they're gifts from God.

Take a Bow...44
See the different gifts God gives to each person.

A Cord of Three..44
Find out about the help that God promises to those he loves.

Building Esteem From Child to Self

Yarn Circle 48
Children realize that they are special people.

The "Special" Game..48
Children find out they're special even when they goof.

I Like Me! 49
Recognize qualities they like about themselves.

Do You Wish?...49
Children learn that God made them just right.

Special Things About Us.......................................50
Children write special things under pictures of themselves.

Let's Pretend 50
Children imagine what family members appreciate about them.

I Am Special 51
Learn what it means to be a unique creation of God.

Love Loops 51
Make decorative necklaces that represent the children's special qualities.

Super Kids...52
     Children bring in and display things they're proud of.

My Me Box 52
     Children decorate boxes and fill them with things
             that represent their interests.

Flower Power...53
     Fill the room with colored flowers that show children's accomplishments.

You Are Special..55
     Recognize the qualities children have inside that make them special.

Publish It...55
     Watch children's self-esteem grow when they see their writing in print.

Armor March..56
     See how God provides protection for his special people.

Guess What I'm Good At...57
     Children act out what others are good at.

Success Ladder...57
     Make ladders that show achievements children are proud of.

Birthday Bonanza 58
     Pick something special about themselves for every year they've been alive.

Hear Ye! Hear Ye! I Am Great!.....................................59
     Each child announces to the class why he or she is great.

Student Authors 60
     Children write and design books to teach younger children Bible truths.

Building Esteem From Child to Child

Who's Out?...62
     Choose to affirm a classmate or leave the game.

Wear the Crown..62
     Each child becomes King or Queen for the Day.

Start With a Song..63
     Sing a song for each classmate.

I'd Like to Give You a Hand..64
     Give one another construction paper hands for accomplishments.

Warm Gifts..64
     Write hidden messages that tell good things about themselves.

Three Cheers for Us 65
     Give a cheer for each classmate.

Thumbs Up 65
     Watch one another during class to see praiseworthy actions.

Builder Uppers 66
     Build a tower that represents unique qualities about a partner.

Trading Places...66
     Play a Musical Chairs variation to affirm one another.

Give a Cheer 67
     Make pompons to cheer for each classmate.

Class Handshake...68
     Create a special handshake and teach it to each new class member.

Peer Interviews 68
     Show their interest by interviewing their classmates.

Practicing Love..69
     Tape-record positive messages about one another.

Listen...69
     Show they care by listening to one another.

Silver-Boxed Boost..70
Give a gift and share a compliment.

Talent Scouts 70
Travel to see each person's special event.

You're Beary Nice..71
Notice positive traits with this beary fun activity.

Love Notes..73
Send love messages to each class member.

It's All in Your Name..73
Write complimentary phrases that begin with
the letters of each person's first name.

Building Bricks 74
Paint bricks with good traits to teach building one another up.

Kindness Gifts 75
Give gifts of kindness to one another.

Secret Admirers 75
Send postcards with affirmations from secret pals.

"Guess Who" Surveys 76
Choose a Mystery Person for the Day and tell him or her, "You're special."

Chains of Friendship 77
Make a never-ending chain of encouragement.

Special Notes Board 77
Have children leave kind notes for one another on a bulletin board.

Write and Rub..78
Write special messages on a partner's back.

Juicy Fruit..79
Decide which fruit of the Spirit each child displays.

Pinky Links..80
    Make the link between friends stronger as they share strengths.

Heavy Burdens...80
Children show their regard for classmates by offering to carry their burdens.

Fire Power 81
    Affirm one another with a meaningful candle-lighting activity.

Building Esteem From Child to Others

Praise Him, Praise Him...84
    Change the words of a familiar song to praise others.

Thumb Books...84
    Send a personalized greeting to show others they're appreciated.

Prayer Grams 85
    Children build others up with prayer.

Helping Hands 86
    Prepare awards to show others their efforts are appreciated.

Get Well Soon..86
    Send a unique get well card full of "holy kisses."

Hug Club...87
    Spread hugs, joy and appreciation with this one.

Chalk It Up 88
    Create sidewalk chalk affirmations.

Smiles Are Catching...88
    Have children greet churchgoers as they arrive.

Secret Person of the Month..89
    Choose a person to appreciate all month long.

Flowers Say It Best 90
    Make a bouquet of tissue paper flowers to give away.

People Who Serve God 91
    Play Charades to recognize church members who serve.

We're Nuts About You 91
    Thank adult helpers in a fun and unique way.

All Puffed Up 92
    Children learn to build others up instead of bragging about themselves.

Introduction

"Why do you always...?"
"Why can't you...?"
"I just wish that for once you'd..."
"No, that's not the way to do it."

Think how discouraging it is for children to put their best into a project only to be told their efforts simply don't measure up.

It's only a matter of time before children begin to think the problem is that *they* aren't very good. Such children give up on themselves.

Sadly, when a child's potential goes untapped or is stunted by a lack of self-esteem, the child's unique abilities are lost forever because there will never be another creation just like that child.

As adults who work with children, our charge and opportunity is to nurture children so they can become the individuals God meant them to be.

There's no doubt about it. God has great things planned for each child in your care. Paul tells us that we are created to do good works in Christ. David marvels that we are fearfully and wonderfully made. And perhaps what is most astounding is that scripture tells us we are derived from God.

This book is a powerful tool for teaching children that they are special creations.

In *Esteem-Builders for Children's Ministry*, you'll find plenty of fun-filled activities for preschoolers to sixth-graders that'll teach them they're special. These crafts, games and projects will encourage children to recognize their abilities and stretch their potential.

In the first section, "Building Esteem From Teacher to

Child," you'll find lots of tips to show children they matter to you in and beyond the classroom.

The activities in "Building Esteem From God to Child" will let children know that the Creator of the universe has a deep and personal love for each of them.

In "Building Esteem From Child to Self," children will learn to love themselves and find motivation to accomplish great things.

"Building Esteem From Child to Child" will give children the chance to appreciate their peers.

The book's last section, "Building Esteem From Child to Others," will teach children to applaud the efforts and gifts of those outside their own classrooms and to encourage others in a biblical way.

Use this resource often to build confidence in your children. And remember, *you* have abilities, gifts and insights that can be used to show God's love for each child in a way that no one else can!

wow
wonderful
best
incredible
AMAZING
excellent
SUPER
cool
Yea!
awesome
TERRIFIC
amazing

cool

incredible

Yeah

AWESOME

TERRIFIC

Building Esteem
From Teacher
to Child

wow

GREAT

fantastic

Willy Worm

Here's a way to make children feel better when things aren't going their way. Introduce the class to Willy Worm. Use a pen to draw two eyes and a smile on the end of your index finger. Tell the class that Willy doesn't like to see unhappy people. Whenever Willy sees children who are unhappy, he'll give them worm hugs.

When you notice a child's frustration or disappointment (maybe Josh spilled his juice or Regina can't make the scissors work), tell him or her that Willy thinks a worm hug is necessary. Hold the child's hand gently and lightly tickle his or her palm with Willy. You're sure to be rewarded with a smile.

Just Because

Welcome the children as they enter the room and place a sticker on the back of each child's hand. Make sure every child receives a sticker, but don't tell the children why they received the stickers.

Later in class, ask:
- Who got a sticker?
- Why do you think you received it?

Say: **Today everybody got a sticker just because. You didn't get one because you *did* anything special. I wanted to give each of you a sticker because you *are* special. Each of you is special to me and to God.**

The Kindness Worm

Use a sock to make a simple worm puppet. Sew or glue on buttons and fabric scraps to decorate the worm, or color it with markers. In the bottom of a round basket, put a hole big enough for your forearm to fit through. Keep the worm puppet in the basket.

Tell the children that they can persuade the worm out of its basket by being especially kind to others. When you notice praiseworthy behavior, get out the worm's basket. Secretly slip your hand in the sock. If you hold the basket with your other arm, it'll look like the worm is coming out of the basket. Have the worm thank the child who persuaded it out of the basket with his or her kind action.

Animal Goodbyes

Try one of these when your children leave for the day.
Elephant Kisses—Pull your shirt sleeve down so that it extends about 2 inches below your fingertips. Kiss each child with the floppy shirt-sleeve trunk.

Fish Faces—Kiss goodbye through a glass door or window. Show children how to make fish faces. Let your "fish" lips touch the "aquarium" glass as you say goodbye. If children give you fish kisses back, make sure you clean the glass between kisses!

Creepy-Crawly Goodbyes—Lightly run your fingers along each child's inner forearm from wrist to elbow.

I Love You in Lots of Languages

Preschool-3

Children are intrigued with other languages and cultures. Use these expressions of love any time to let them know they're special.

Spanish—*te amor* (sounds like tay ahmo)
French—*Je t'aime* (sounds like je tem)
German—*Ich liebe Dich* (sounds like ick leeba deek)
Italian—*lo tiamo* (sounds like yo teeahmo)
And even pig Latin—I-ay ove-lay ou-yay

You're Great!

Preschool-3

Try some of these silly ways to celebrate outstanding accomplishments or just to celebrate having special kids.

● Let children shoot baskets with a Nerf ball and a hoop fastened to the wall.

● Sprinkle drops of water on children's heads.

● Let children get gum balls from a gum-ball machine.

● Order sets of sample foreign stamps and hand them out.

● Have a jar of bubbles handy so children can blow bubbles.

● Write, "Great job!" on the backs of children's hands.

● Save Easter egg decals and let children use them as tattoos.

● Put a drop of lemon or vanilla extract on the backs of children's hands for them to smell.

Encouraging Words

Preschool–4

As children are working on projects in class, encourage them with statements such as "I like the yellow color you've chosen, Sally" or "You're using just the right amount of glue, Kyle." Find something nice to say about each child. Pat them on their backs or just place your hand on their shoulders as you talk to them.

When they've finished their work, tell them how proud you are of the hard work they've done.

Spare Hugs

Preschool–4

Before the children go home, ask them if they have any spare hugs. You just may be bombarded with bearhugs. Say: **I love you and so does Jesus.**

Growing

Preschool–4

Help children plant rapidly growing seeds, such as carrot or grass seeds, into small, individual pots, such as plastic-foam cups. Don't explain why they've planted the seeds.

Watch your students' activities in class so you'll be prepared to write a special note for each child. Cut out small squares of construction paper. On the front write, "You're growing more like Jesus every day." On the back write a special action that you've observed, such as "Thank you, Christopher, for making our new student feel welcome" or "Thank you, Annie, for staying after class to help clean up." Tape or glue a toothpick to the note, and

stick it in the dirt of a pot.
When the seedlings surface, send a pot home with each child.

The Very Important People Book

Preschool-4

At the beginning of the year, take pictures of all your students. Also take candid shots showing the class singing, working on art projects and playing games.

When the pictures are developed, mount them in a book. Use a paint pen to write, "The Very Important People Book" on the cover. Add captions and include a list of children's names, addresses and phone numbers. Be sure to get permission from parents before you list children's addresses and phone numbers. Some parents prefer to keep this information confidential.

Each time your class meets, send the book home with a different child. Make sure children know they're responsible to return the book the next time you meet.

The book is a good way to help reinforce the friendships that are made in class. And, when new children join the class, the book will help introduce them to the people and routines of your class.

Keep in Touch

Listen to the children in your class. Find out what they're doing and what they like. For example, if Nathan tells Brian about the soccer game on Thursday, make a mental note to ask Nathan next Sunday how his soccer game came out. If he wins, say, "That's great. I bet it was a fun game." If he loses, say, "That's okay. I bet you had fun anyway."

Keep in touch with your children even when they aren't in your classroom. You'll be surprised how much it means to them and to you.

Take a Little Time

Preschool-6

At least twice a year, take time to visit each child in his or her home. Bring samples of the child's work and chat with the parents about what your class does to learn about God. Have the child show you his or her room and introduce you to his or her brothers and sisters.

Be sure you mention to the parents how much you enjoy having the child in class.

Missing Children

Preschool-6

Each time a child is missing from class, send that child a card stating that you missed him or her. A good resource is Children's Ministry Care Cards™: Attendance-Builders, which is available from Group Publishing, Box 481, Loveland, CO 80539. There are six designs in the 30-card packet. The cards

21

include messages such as "Jump in and join us" and "We need you to make our group complete."

If a child misses more than a couple of Sundays in a row, give him or her a telephone call. Don't express disapproval about the absence, but tell the child how much you missed seeing him or her. Find out if there's a problem that makes it difficult for the child to attend church. You could even offer to pick up the child next week.

When children return to your class after missing a week or two, tell them how glad you are to see them again.

Candid Camera

Preschool-6

Use a camera to catch children in the act of demonstrating their faith. You might take pictures of children taking turns on the playground or helping one another put on their coats.

Mount the pictures and write appropriate captions on the bulletin board for everyone to see. Your title might be "Candid Camera Caught You Acting Like Christ." Be sure to send captioned pictures home so that parents can add their praise to yours.

There's a Flower in You

K-3

For this activity you'll need to gather several packets of flower seeds and a bouquet of several kinds of flowers in bloom. Choose wildflowers or weeds from a field, flowers from your garden or an inexpensive bouquet from the grocery store. Make sure you have a bloom and a seed for each child. You'll also need a small envelope for each child.

Empty the seed packets into a small bowl. Put the bouquet next to the bowl of seeds.

Have the children sit on the floor in a circle. Show them the seeds and the bouquet. Say: **Look at these flower seeds in this bowl. When you plant these seeds in the ground and water them, they grow to be flowers like these.**

Ask:
- **What else can you do with a seed?** If children are stumped by the question, tell them that some seeds are good to eat, such as pumpkin seeds and sunflower seeds. Other possibilities for using seeds include gluing them to paper to make a picture or sewing them in a bag to make a bean bag. Encourage creative and unusual responses to this question.

Ask:
- **What can you do with a flower?** Again, there are lots of good answers to this question. Encourage children's ideas. Children might say make pictures with them, eat them or give them to a friend.

Ask:
- **If you could pick, would you rather be a seed or a flower?**

Say: **I have good news for you. You don't have to pick because all of you are like both the seed and the flower. The small seed is like all the things you can do as a child. The big flower is like all the things you'll be able to do when you grow up. Seeds and flowers are different just like children and grown-ups are different. But God made each to be a very special part of the world.**

Ask:
- **What can you do now as a child?** Have children act out their responses. They might say ride a bike, run fast or read well.
- **What will you do when you become an adult?** Have children act out their responses. They might say drive a car, be an astronaut or be president.

Give each child a seed in an envelope and a bloom to take home.

I'm Thinking

K-3

This guessing game is good for boosting children's self-esteem without them even knowing it. Once you get to know the children, you'll be able to pick up on their accomplishments and attributes.

The objective is for you to describe one of the children while everyone tries to guess who it is. Start by giving positive attributes, followed by more details so the children can narrow down their choices to guess the person.

For example, say, "I am thinking of someone who is good in soccer, waits his turn to talk, is polite to his parents, and is wearing blue pants and a striped shirt."

The more positive things you can say about each child the better. Guessing the person correctly is secondary to the children hearing positive statements about themselves.

If a child guesses incorrectly, say, "You're right, that child does have all these traits, but I'm thinking of someone else. Keep listening for more clues."

Golden Apple Delight

K-3

Remind children how important their words are. Photocopy the apple from the next page on to yellow paper. Encourage them to drop negative words, such as "stupid," from their vocabulary. Read Proverbs 25:11, "The right word spoken at the right time is as beautiful as gold apples in a silver bowl."

Tell the children that you'll be watching them and if you catch someone using kind words, such as "You're my friend" or "Thank you," you'll award that person a yellow paper apple to pin to his or her shirt.

Caring Cats

Make enough photocopies of the cat on the next page for each child. Make a few extras for visitors and newcomers. Cover a bulletin board with colorful paper and write, "We Are Caring Cats" at the top.

Have each child cut out a cat and decorate it with markers, glitter and paper scraps. You may need to help younger children use scissors.

Have children each put their name on their cat. Attach a 2-foot tail of thick, gift-wrap yarn to the cat. Mount cats on the bulletin board with tacks.

Every time you see a child being kind or helpful, silently go to the bulletin board and tie a knot in the tail of that child's cat. Watch to see that every child receives knots. Have children each take home their cat when its tail is full of knots.

27

We Miss You When You're Gone

You'll need construction paper, scissors, markers, posterboard and tape. Make a large flower petal for children to trace. Refer to the shape below.

Have children take turns tracing the flower petal onto construction paper. Have them each cut out their petal and put their name on it with their favorite color.

On a sheet of posterboard, draw a circle for a flower center and a long stem with leaves. Refer to the illustration.

Have children tape their petals with one end touching the flower center. Some petals may overlap if your class is large, but make sure the tip of each petal is visible.

After all the petals are in place, remove a petal here and there. Say: **Look what happens to the flower when Emily, Mark and Dennis aren't here. The flower has empty spaces. Each of you is very important in our class. I know that you can't**

always come, but we miss you when you're gone.

Have children say what they miss about each person when he or she is absent from class. For example, Mark might say, "When Dennis is gone, I miss talking about football games."

Have the children take home their flower petals as a reminder of how important they are to the class.

Decisions, Decisions

When you have decisions to make that involve the class, such as what kind of snack to have or what to do for a fun outing, make sure you share the decision-making power with the children. This tells children that they really do count.

Spotlights

Give each child in your class the opportunity to stand in the spotlight. Work with children's parents to collect objects or pictures of objects that represent each child's interests, such as sports equipment, instruments, art projects, favorite foods, pets, favorite books, collections, awards, trophies and favorite scripture verses. Make sure that none of the items chosen would embarrass a child.

Each week, put a different child in the spotlight. Display his or her objects on a table covered with a cloth in the child's favorite color. Also, present pictures from the different stages of the child's life. Let the other children look at the display before or after class.

Interview the Flock

Get to know your students with this survey! This activity works best when the children are busy with other teachers or workers. Select one child at a time for a private interview. Choose a different child each time your class meets. Make sure you interview each child.

When you and the child are alone, tell the child that you want to get to know him or her better. Ask the child the questions in the box below. Photocopy the list of questions to make the interview easier. Take your time during the interview and feel free to change the questions as much as you want. The idea is to show the children that you're sincerely interested in them.

At the end of the interview, tell the child something that you find special about him or her. Hold the child's hand and pray out loud for that child's life, safety and growth in Christ. Tell the child that you're always available to talk and make sure to follow through with your promise.

Questions:

1. How old are you?
2. What grade are you in?
3. What is your favorite subject or activity at school? Why?
4. What is your favorite food?
5. Do you have any brothers and sisters? How old are they, and what are their names?
6. Do you have pets? If so, what are they like?
7. What is the most fun thing that you can remember doing?
8. What kinds of things make you really mad?
9. If you could go anywhere in the world, where would you go? Why?
10. What would you like to be when you grow up? Why?
11. What kinds of things do you like to do with your free time? Tell me more about that.
12. What do you like and dislike about church? Why?
13. Is there anything you'd like to ask about me?

30

Whose Birthday Is It, Anyway?

K-6

Send cards to all the children on *your* birthday instead of on theirs, with a note about what they mean to you and how important their friendship is to you and to the class.

Half Birthdays

K-6

Everyone expects a little attention on his or her birthday, so surprise students in your class by recognizing them on their half birthdays. Find out each child's birthday, add six months and you'll have each child's half birthday!

During the class meeting closest to the person's half birthday, have the class form a circle around him or her. Say: **You're special to us, and we love you.** Have the children in the class each share one thing they admire about the person, such as the child's Bible knowledge or the fun way he or she participates in games. Then sing "Happy Half Birthday to You."

Cookie Kisses

K-6

Treat your class to cookie kisses that look like giant Hershey's Kisses. Mix up a batch of Rice Krispies treats according to the recipe on the cereal box. Instead of pushing the mixture into one pan, divide it into cookie-sized mounds.

Make enough mounds for every child in your class, plus a few extra.

Grease a small kitchen funnel with butter or margarine and use it as a cookie mold. Push each cookie-sized mound into the funnel. The cookie will fall right out when you turn the funnel upside down. You may need to regrease the funnel periodically to keep the cookie mixture from sticking.

Make strips of paper that are about twice as long as the diameter of the base of the cookies. Make enough strips for each child to have one. On each strip of paper, write a child's name and something special about him or her. Make a few generic kisses for visitors. These kisses could say, "We're especially glad you came today" or "Your smile brightens our classroom."

Wrap each cookie kiss in foil, inserting a slip of paper in the top so the child's name extends beyond the foil.

Pass out the cookies and have children eat them at snack time. Read the messages out loud. Be sure to send the messages home so parents can reinforce your words of praise.

The Barnabas Connection

1-6

Barnabas was a great help to Paul. Read Acts 11:22-30. Do you have a helper and encourager like Barnabas in your class? Maybe you have more than one who is always ready and eager to help.

Instead of affirming individuals for their help in front of everyone, make the "Barnabas Connection" in secret. Recognize a child's helpfulness by slipping a secret note to him or her after class. Keep it a secret between the two of you.

In your note, say: **I am so thankful God has put you in my class. Your help is very much appreciated. You are very special to God and to me.**

Mirror Writing

Write an individual mirror message to each child in your class. Mirror messages are written backward so that they must be held up to a mirror to be read correctly. Here's an easy way to do it.

On a sheet of white paper, write out the alphabet in capital and lowercase block letters with a thick marker that'll bleed through the paper. You'll also want to write several punctuation symbols, such as a comma, a question mark and quotation marks. Be sure to put something under the paper you're writing on to protect the table from the marker.

Then turn over the sheet of paper so you can see where the marker bled through. Fill in any letters that didn't bleed through completely. This will be your key so you can know how the letters look backward. To check your work on the key, hold it up to the mirror. The reflection should read correctly.

Next, compose your messages to the children. You might want to recognize children for accomplishments in class. For example, "Dear Sandy, I saw you helping Brian with his art project. Great work!"

Don't forget to write from *right* to *left*. Double-check all your messages by holding them up to a mirror before you give them to the children.

Pass the messages out as the children are leaving. Tell the children to hold the messages up to a mirror at home.

33

wow

wonderfu

best

incredible

AMAZING

excellent

SUPER

cool

Ve

awesome   TERRIFIC   buizpw

Building Esteem
From
God to Child

One Lost Sheep

Preschool-3

Before class, photocopy and cut out 10 sheep. Hide the sheep in the classroom. Put one sheep in a very difficult-to-find hiding place.

Say: **Let's be shepherds and look for 10 lost sheep.** Encourage children to hunt for the sheep even if they get discouraged when one is hard to find.

Read Luke 15:3-6 to the class.

Ask:

● **Why did the shepherd keep looking for the one lost sheep?**

● **How do you think the sheep felt when the shepherd kept looking?**

● **How do you think the sheep would've felt if the shepherd had given up because it was too hard to find?**

Say: **The shepherd loved that sheep just as much as all of the other sheep, so he kept looking until he found it. God loves us as much as the shepherd loved that lost sheep. God promises to take care of us just like the shepherd took care of the sheep.**

Give each child a sheep to take home. Photocopy more sheep, if necessary.

Guess Who God Loves

B efore class, secure a mirror to the bottom of a deep box that has a lid. Then close the box. During class, say: **In this box I have a picture of someone God loves. God believes this person can do very important things. What's exciting is that each one of you knows this person.**

As the children's curiosity is piqued, ask:

● **Whose picture do you think is in here?**

As each child makes a guess, let him or her peek in the box to see who God loves. Tell them not to tell anyone else who they saw. Once all the children have peeked, ask if they were surprised by who they saw.

Pray: **Dear God, thank you for loving each of us. Thank you for watching over us and always being ready to help us. Thank you for making each one of us special and important. Amen.**

Take the mirror out of the box and hang it on a wall in your classroom at the children's eye level. Above the mirror put the words, "God loves…" Encourage the children often to look in the mirror to see who God loves.

Jesus Loves You

P lay this version of Duck, Duck, Goose to let children know Jesus loves them. Have children sit in a circle and choose a volunteer to be "It." It walks around the circle tapping each child's head. Instead of saying, "Duck, duck, duck, duck, GOOSE," he or she says, "Jesus loves, loves, loves, YOU!" When It touches a child's head and says "you," the child jumps up and chases It around the circle. It must try to run around the circle and get back to the child's place without getting tagged. If It makes it around the circle without getting tagged, the child becomes the new It. If It does get tagged, he or she takes another turn at being It and the game begins again.

Play until everyone gets a turn—because Jesus really does love everyone in the circle.

This Is Our Class

K-4

On a large sheet of posterboard, write, "We're all different, but God loves each of us just the way we are." Use a video camera to videotape the poster while you read it aloud.

Then videotape each child individually while you ask, **"What's your name?" "How old are you?" "Where do you go to school?"** and **"What's your favorite thing to do on Saturday?"**

Then videotape the poster and read it aloud once again.

Set up a television and a VCR. Then view the videotape with the children. Children are likely to giggle when they see one another on television.

The Seal of the King

For this one you'll need a candle for every five students, matches and an ornate ring. Look for an inexpensive ring at the jewelry counter or in the toy department of discount stores. You'll also need square-shaped pieces of paper and markers.

Light the candles early in the meeting to allow plenty of wax to melt. Give children each a square piece of paper and have them write or draw one of God's promises on their paper. For example, Jerry might write, "God answers my prayers." Then have children fold each corner in toward the center of their pieces of paper so that the four corners meet.

Tell the children that when people in Bible times received messages from the ruler of their country, they knew the message was truly from their king because it was sealed with his ring.

Say: **God has made lots of promises to us because he loves us. Let's pretend that this ring is God's emblem, and let's seal these promises with the emblem to remind us that these messages come from God.**

Dribble a small amount of wax onto each child's piece of paper where the corners meet. Wait a moment for the wax to set up. Have children work quickly to press the ring into the wax before the wax hardens completely. Tell the children that when they're having a hard time, they can open their "envelopes" and read the message of the King.

40

Sweet-Smelling Acts

You'll need a bottle of spray perfume or a can of air freshener. Write acts of Christian witness such as kindness, gentleness and self-control on slips of paper and hide them around the room. On some of the slips, write down things you've seen the children do, such as choosing not to cheat or sharing an answer to prayer.

Read 2 Corinthians 2:14-15. Show children the perfume. Tell the children to hunt for the slips. When a child finds a slip, have the class stop hunting while the child reads it aloud and sprays one squirt of the sweet smell into the air away from faces.

When all the strips have been found, say: **When you do these things, you're like a beautiful fragrance that God uses to show people about his love.**

As a take-home goodie, spray some of the fragrance on fabric swatches or on pieces of heavy paper.

God Loves Me Go-Around

Have the children sit in a circle on the floor or in chairs, and take turns finishing the sentence, "God loves my..." Give an example to get the game started, such as "God loves my smile." Be ready to give ideas to those who can't think of anything.

Keep going around the circle taking turns and going progressively faster until you're going so fast there's not much time to think between answers. Continue until the children run out of ideas.

Rainbows

Have the children form a circle. Give each child a crayon. Try not to duplicate colors. Draw a large arch on a big sheet of paper and put it on the floor in the center of the circle. One by one, have the children draw an arch under yours with their colors. When they are finished, hold up the rainbow.

Say: **When we started this picture, all anyone had was one color. Now we have a rainbow. Each color added more beauty to the first. God gave us the colors of a rainbow to enjoy, just as he gave us one another to enjoy.**

Then have the class members each pass their crayon to the person on their right, telling them how much they enjoy knowing them.

Say: **God also gave us rainbows as reminders that he would never forget us. We're all very special to him and to one another. Let's remember this as we work together in class.**

Reflecting God's Light

1-6

You'll need a mirror and a flashlight. Place the mirror in the center of the floor space. Have children form a circle around it.

Pass the flashlight around the circle. Say: **When the flashlight comes to you, shine it so the light bounces off the mirror. Then tell one way you can reflect God's light.**

When all the children have shared, take the flashlight and shine it on each one as you pray a prayer of thanksgiving for that person's ability to shine for Jesus.

A Gift From God

1-6

You will need scraps of wrapping paper, tape and miniature gift-bows for this activity.

Give each child a scrap of wrapping paper about 3×4 inches. Show children how to fold the paper into fifths and tape two of the sections together to form a square tube. It'll look like a present with both ends

open. Have children tape gift bows on their "presents."

Then have children form a circle. Have them each turn to the person on their right, slip the present on the person's finger and say, "You're a gift from God."

Take a Bow

1-6

G ive each child a self-adhesive gift bow. Form groups of four. In the groups, have each child share something he or she does particularly well, such as writing songs or drawing pictures. Have children each say to the child on their right, "I believe God can use your gift of..." and then stick a gift bow on his or her shoulder. Read 1 Corinthians 12:4-6. Say: **In God's family, we have all been given different gifts. Let's thank God for our differences.**

A Cord of Three

4-6

F or this activity you'll need thread. Give children each a 12-inch piece of thread and challenge them to break it. Most will be able to do so with a little bit of effort.

Have children form pairs. Give each child a new section of thread. Have partners twist their threads together and then try to break them.

Then give each pair three pieces of thread. Have each pair tie the threads together at one end and braid them. Have them tie the other ends together after the three threads are braided together. Have each pair try to break the braided cord.

Ask:

● **When you were trying to break the threads, when was it easiest? when was it hardest?**

Read Ecclesiastes 4:9-12.

Ask:
● How is the strength of the braided cord like having God and friends to help you stand up to troubles?

Say: When you face difficult circumstances, a friend's help and God are an unbreakable combination. And what's even better is that God promises to stick by us and strengthen us. He'll never leave us because he loves us.

Building Esteem
From
Child to Self

Yarn Circle

Use a piece of yarn to make a circle on the floor that's big enough for all the children to stand in. Make the circle small enough that children will have to stand close together. Have the children stand around the yarn circle about four or five feet back.

Say: **This circle is for a special person in this room. Let's find out who belongs in the special circle.**

God loves the special person in our class. If God loves you, take one step toward the circle.

This person is different from anyone else in the world. If there's something about you that makes you different from everybody else, take one step toward the circle.

This person likes to laugh and have fun. If you like to laugh, take one step toward the circle.

Sometimes, this person makes mistakes and gets into trouble. But this person can learn from mistakes. If you make mistakes sometimes, take one step toward the circle.

This special person knows how to do lots of things. If you can think of something you know how to do like jumping on one foot across the room, take one step toward the circle.

By this time, everyone should be inside the circle. Say: **Look at all the special people we have in our classroom. I'm glad I made the circle big enough for all of you.**

The "Special" Game

This game will remind you of Simon Says, but it's more *special* than that. The children must follow your actions, but only when you say all three words of "If you're special" first.
Say: **If you're special—hug yourself!** Demonstrate the action

by wrapping your arms around yourself.

When all the children hug themselves, you might hop on one foot and say, "You're special—hop on one foot!" Oops! You left out the word "if"!

Tell all hopping children to repeat after you, "I goofed, but I'm special anyway!"

Continue playing for several minutes.

I Like Me!

Have children sit in a circle on the floor. Chant the words below. When you get to the blank, fill it in with something you like about yourself, such as the color of your hair or your ability to ride a bike. Have children join in the chant. Each time you come to the blank, have a different child fill it in with something positive about him- or herself.

I like me,
I like me,
I like me, because _____.

Add hand clapping and finger snapping to keep the rhythm going.

Do You Wish?

Choose a volunteer to begin this game. Whisper in his or her ear to act like an elephant with a long trunk. Let the child choose the best way to act this out. Have the rest of the children guess what animal the volunteer is acting out.

Then ask:

● **Would you like to be an elephant with a long trunk?**

Have all the children pretend to be elephants with long trunks. Let the volunteer lead a procession of all the elephants around the room. Then say: **It might be fun to be an elephant with a long trunk, but God made you a person.**

Have the children respond by saying, "I'm glad I'm me!"

Continue with volunteers acting out a rabbit with big ears, a butterfly with beautiful wings, a crocodile with sharp teeth, a monkey jumping in a tree and a squirrel with a bushy tail.

End by saying: **I'm glad you're you, too. I think God made you just right!**

Special Things About Us

Preschool–2

Select a bulletin board in your classroom or make one out of a large sheet of cardboard. Take pictures of all the children and yourself.

Mount each picture on the board with enough room to write something special about each person. Have children add things about themselves or others.

Leave the bulletin board up for a few months or until there is no more space to add new ideas.

As you are adding items, make sure everyone has something to add. Remind the children that little things, like helping someone, being polite or saying your prayers are very special to God. You don't have to receive awards to be special.

Remember to share the board with any guests and parents to show off the class's special characteristics.

Let's Pretend

K–2

This is a good activity to do in the beginning of the year to get to know the children in your class. Say: **Let's pretend that I've sneaked into your house, and I'm standing in your kitchen doorway. Your family is in the kitchen, and they're** saying two special things about you. **What will I hear them say?**

Go around the room, and have children each tell you two good things about themselves. Don't forget to include yourself in the sharing.

End by saying: **Your family thinks you're special and so do I. God also thinks you're special.**

I Am Special

K-2

Give each child a large paper bag. Have them each fold the bag from the bottom so it fits over their head and rests on their shoulders.

Now have each child draw nose and eye holes, and cut them out. Have the children place their masks over their heads, making sure they can see.

Have children pretend that everyone is just alike. Have them move around the room like robots.

Now tell them they're about to see some of God's magic. Have them remove their masks and look at one another. Talk about how each person has two eyes, a nose and a mouth, yet each person looks different. If there are identical twins in your class, talk about how they're different even though they look similar.

Love Loops

K-3

For this activity, you'll need 24-inch lengths of yarn, a box of circle-shaped cereal, such as Froot Loops, and bowls. Give each child a length of yarn and a piece of cereal to string on the yarn. Say: **This loop represents God's love for you. God made you very special. Can you think of reasons that you are special?**

Some children may need help thinking of reasons. Get them

started by mentioning a special quality about each of them.

Set bowls of cereal around the room and have the children keep stringing pieces of cereal on their yarn lengths for each reason that they're special. Continue until the yarn strands are full or until you run out of cereal. Tie the ends of the yarn together and have the children wear their esteem necklaces with pride throughout the class session.

Have the children wear their necklaces home, and encourage children to explain to their parents why they're special.

Super Kids

K-4

Cover a bulletin board with paper and write the words, "Super Kids" at the top. Encourage children to bring in items that show accomplishments they're proud of; for example, school papers, report cards or artwork. Put paper out for children to draw or to write about accomplishments, such as learning to ride a bicycle.

Post children's accomplishments on the bulletin board.

Some children may not think they've done anything worth acknowledging. Help these children think of achievements to be proud of. Make sure every child is represented on the bulletin board.

Display the items for a month, but encourage children to bring in new items at any time.

My Me Box

K-4

Give children each a shoe box. Have them decorate their boxes to represent themselves, using items such as paints, markers, wrapping paper, glitter, magazine pictures and pictures of themselves.

Have the children take their boxes home and fill them with items that are special. Children may choose to put favorite baseball cards, toys or souvenirs in their boxes.

Have children bring their boxes to the next class meeting. Have children each show and tell about their box and the items inside.

Flower Power   K-4

Make a flower garden poster by using the pattern on the next page to trace lots of flowers on a sheet of newsprint or posterboard.

Give children a few minutes when they arrive to color a flower for an accomplishment they're proud of, such as cleaning up classroom supplies without being told to or finishing a school project that took a lot of effort. Ask them about what they've accomplished.

When the poster is full, begin a new one. By the end of the year, your entire room will look like a flower garden of accomplishments.

54

You Are Special

K-4

Give each child an apple to examine.

Ask:
● **What's special about apples?**

Encourage children's creative responses—the more unusual the better.

Say: **There's a secret inside every apple that you can't see unless you cut it open. Watch to see what it is.**

Cut open one of the apples not from top to bottom, but from side to side. The core of the apple will look like a star.

Ask:
● **What makes you special on the inside?**
● **What is special about you that nobody can see?**

Cut sheets of construction paper each into three lengthwise strips. Give each child a paper strip. Put thick tempera paint in shallow pans. Have the children dip one of the cut apple pieces into the paint and stamp it on their paper strips. If you have more than six children, cut another apple in half for the children to use as a stamp. Have them write their names on their strips. Set the strips aside to dry.

Then have children each write on their strip one thing that makes them special. Children who can't write can draw pictures.

Publish It

K-6

All children love seeing their names in print. If you have a church newsletter, encourage your children to write something for it. First, talk with whoever's in charge of the newsletter to make sure submissions from children are welcome.

Children could write poems, stories or puzzles. Children who are too young to write could draw illustrations for older children's stories. Make sure bylines are included with each submission.

If children aren't interested in writing, write about your class.

Write a monthly update on what the class is doing. Include children's names and any special projects they're working on.

If a published newsletter is not available, you could create your own handout. Older children could rewrite Bible stories for younger children, or a handout could be made for parents. Again, include bylines whenever possible.

Don't worry about making the design of the handout too professional. Use a marker to put the name of your newsletter at the top of a piece of typing paper. Type the children's stories under the name of the newsletter. Let the children create illustrations and use a glue stick to put them under or beside the stories. Then photocopy as many as you need.

Don't forget the local newspaper. They often welcome contributions from children. Let the people at the newspaper office know when you're working on a large project, such as a food drive. Often, newspapers will print such stories free, and they may even send a photographer and a reporter to your classroom.

Armor March

C hildren will feel good about themselves when they know how God prepares them to face the world. To get them started, lead them in this armor march based on Ephesians 6:13-18.

Have the children act out these motions as if they were marching in an army. Your role is to act as the general, barking the following orders and acting them out as an example to the troops. Say:

- Attention! March 2-3-4!
- Buckle the belt of truth around your waist, and march 2-3-4!
- Put on the chest protector of right living, and march 2-3-4!
- Put the good-news-of-peace shoes on your feet, and march 2-3-4!
- Pick up the shield of faith to block the fiery darts of the enemy, and march 2-3-4!

- Put on the helmet of God's salvation, and march 2-3-4!
- Pull out the sword of the Spirit, which is God's Word, and march 2-3-4!
- Bow in prayer, then march 2-3-4!
- Be ready and watchful, and march 2-3-4!
- Company halt! Stand your ground!

Guess What I'm Good At
2-4

Have children each write on a slip of paper their name and something they're good at. Collect all the slips and put them in a bag.

Play a game of Charades by having the children randomly draw the slips of paper and acting them out. As each child draws a name, have him or her say, "This is something (*child's name*) is good at."

End by saying: **I sure have a classroom full of talented people. I never knew you were so good at so many things.**

Pray: **Dear God, thank you for making each of us with special talents. Help us to use them to make the world a better place.**

Success Ladder
2-4

Give each child two 12-inch dowel rods and 12 Popsicle sticks.

On each Popsicle stick, have chil-

dren use a permanent marker to write down an accomplishment they're proud of, such as learning to bake brownies or ride a two-wheel bike.

After children have finished writing on their Popsicle sticks, have them glue the sticks to the two dowel rods to make a ladder.

Set the ladders aside to dry.

The next time class meets, have each child explain his or her success ladder to the rest of the class.

Birthday Bonanza

2-4

Give a sheet of construction paper with a simple drawing of a birthday cake on it to each child. For candles, make paper strips about $1/2$ inch wide and 6 inches long out of bright construction paper. You may want to taper one end of each paper strip to look like the wick end of a candle.

Have the children each choose one candle for each year of their age. For example, an 8-year-old would choose eight candles. Have children each write down one reason they're special on each of their candles. Then have them glue their candles to their birthday cakes. Have them decorate their cakes with torn-paper shapes,

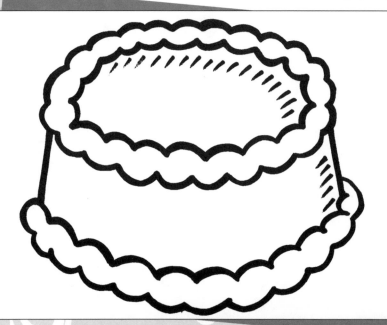

glitter, yarn and other classroom items. Set the cakes aside to dry and then put them away.

On each child's birthday, get out his or her cake and read it aloud to the class. Ask the children to suggest other reasons the birthday child is special. Sing "Happy Birthday to You." Send the cake home with the birthday child.

Hear Ye! Hear Ye! I Am Great! 2–4

Cut a 2×1-foot section of butcher paper for each child. Have children each tape a stick or a dowel rod to each end of their paper.

Have the children write the words, "Hear ye! Hear ye! I am great!" at the top of their papers. Then have them list at least 10 reasons why they're great. Younger children can draw pictures of why they are great.

When their lists are completed, roll the paper around the sticks like scrolls are rolled. Tie pieces of ribbon or yarn around them.

Allow children each to unroll their scroll and read to the class why they're great. Discuss how God made each child very special.

Student Authors

Have children write stories that will help teach younger children about a Bible truth, such as being happy with what you have or trusting God when you're afraid.

Have children each prepare a booklet by folding typing paper and covering it with a decorated sheet of construction paper. Have children each punch holes near the "spine" and tie their booklet together with ribbon.

Be sure to include a page at the end about the author. For example, Jody might write on his own author page:

Jody Sumner was born in Canada on January 1, 1982. He moved to Minnesota in 1985. His favorite color is green. He likes to play basketball and to fish with his grandfather. Last summer he caught a 5-pound catfish. This is his first book, but he has written several poems.

Have the children gift-wrap the booklets and present them to a younger church class.

Building Esteem From Child to Child

Who's Out?

Play this game like Hot Potato. Have children sit in a circle. Tell them to pass around a bean bag or a small ball while you play a tape of lively praise music. When the music stops, whoever is holding the object can either choose to be out of the game or to stay in the game by saying something nice about the person on his or her left.

Discourage children from choosing to be out by saying: **Let's see if we can play the whole game with no one getting out.**

Play until everyone's had a chance to say something nice about someone in the class.

At the end of the game, say: **You're good at this game. It makes me glad to hear you say kind things about one another. It pleases God, too.**

Wear the Crown K-3

Before class, use scissors to scallop one long side on each of two 8½×11 sheets of paper. Then tape together the shorter ends into a circle. This will serve as a crown.

Show the crown to your class. Say: **The Bible tells many stories about kings and queens. Let's choose a King or Queen for the Day.**

Have the children each write their name on a slip of paper and put it in a can. Draw out a name and announce who will be King or Queen for the Day. Put the crown on his or her head.

Hold a special "Interview the King or Queen" session. Let the children ask questions, such as "What's your favorite food?" and "What's your favorite TV show?" You may need to ask a few questions to get the class started.

Let the child wear the crown throughout class and take it home after class. The next time your class meets, make a new crown and draw another name out of the can. Let this child be King or Queen for the Day. Continue until everyone has had a chance at being royalty.

Start With a Song

K-3

Sing this song to the tune of "Frere Jacques." Let children fill in the blank for each child in class so they'll have practice giving as well as receiving compliments. Be sure to include each child each week.

We like Johnny. We like Johnny.
Yes, we do. Yes, we do.
We like our friend Johnny
Because he _____.
He's so kind. He's so kind.

Help children think of ways to affirm one another. Children's ideas may not fit the meter of the song very well. Help them fit their ideas into a three- to five-syllable form. For example, if a child says, "Johnny gave me the yellow crayon today," you might reword it as "We like our friend Johnny/Because he *shares his crayons.*"

I'd Like to Give You a Hand

K-4

Give each child a sheet of construction paper, a pencil and scissors. Have children each trace their hand on the construction paper and cut it out.

When they're finished, have children form a circle. Have each child share one thing he or she feels good about accomplishing, such as learning to tie shoelaces or learning how to multiply. As each child shares, have the person on the child's right say, "I'd like to give you a hand for that" and pass his or her paper hand to the child who shared.

After each child has shared, say: **Let's give each other a hand by clapping.** After they've applauded for one another, say: **Now, let's give God a hand for creating so many gifts and talents among us.**

Warm Gifts

K-6

You'll need white paper, cotton swabs, vinegar, a dry iron and a thick towel. Early in the meeting, give each child a sheet of white paper and a cotton swab. Let them each dip their swab into the vinegar and write or draw something that symbolizes the very best thing about them. Tell them not to put their names on the papers. Set the papers aside to dry.

Either at the end of the meeting or the following week, have each child come to the front of the room, choose one of the sheets of paper and hold a warm, dry iron to it for 30 seconds. Carefully supervise this part of the activity. Protect the surface children iron on with a thick towel.

When the design is revealed, have children guess whose it is. If children can't guess who it belongs to, have the artist identify him- or herself.

Three Cheers for Us

K–6

T he children will cheer for one another when you play this game. Form two teams. The object of this game is for each team to "out-cheer" the other.

This game is played in rounds of competing cheers. Taking turns, each team cheers, "_____, _____! We like _____."

Have each team fill in the blanks with the name of a team member from the opposing team. For example, the first team might choose to cheer for Bob on the other team first. They'd yell, "Bob, Bob! We like Bob." Then the other team chooses a person to cheer. Decide at the end of each round which team shouted the loudest.

Have the teams continue taking turns cheering until all team members on each team have been cheered.

Thumbs Up

K–6

Y ou'll need an ink pad (washable ink is best) for this activity. Secretly assign each child a partner to watch during class. For example, Joanna watches James, James watches Ted and Ted watches Joanna. The children should watch for praiseworthy actions or characteristics, such as helping someone find a Bible passage or helping clean up supplies.

At the end of class, have children each press their thumb on the ink pad, make a thumbprint on the back of their partner's hand and complete this sentence: "I give you the thumbs up for…" For example, Joanna might say to James, "I give you the thumbs up for being excited about praising God during our song time."

Builder Uppers

For this activity, you'll need blocks or Lego building blocks, paper and pencils. Have children form pairs. Give each pair 15 blocks, two sheets of paper and two pencils.

Say: **Each of you has qualities that make you different from everybody else. Have your partner write down something about you that makes you special. Your job is to build a tower with the blocks. Each time your partner writes down something about you, add one block to the tower. Have your partner continue to list qualities until your tower is 15 blocks tall. Then switch roles.**

Have children decide which partner will go first. Then have them play the game.

Afterward, say: **Take home the paper that your partner wrote about you. Look at it throughout the week to remind you that you really are a special creation.**

Trading Places

Make a circle with enough chairs for all the children in your class. Give each child a strip of masking tape and a marker. Or use self-stick notes and markers. Have children each write their name on the tape strip and stick it to the seat of their chair.

Play a cassette tape of praise music and have children walk around the outside of the circle. In the middle of a song, stop the music. When the music stops, children must each sit in the chair closest to them and remove the tape from the chair.

Each person then says something positive about the child whose name he or she has, but doesn't say who the child is. For example, a child might say, "This person always shares" or "This person is lots of fun to play soccer with."

Have the other children guess who the person is. If the class can't guess who it is in three tries, the child who gave the compliment reveals who the person is by sticking the masking tape to the person's back.

Give a Cheer

Have the children each make a pompon by taping colored crepe paper strips to an unsharpened pencil. Demonstrate this cheer with your name before asking children to lead cheers with their own names. For example, say, "Give me a T" (children shout "T" and wave their pompons). "Give me an O" (children shout "O" and wave their pompons). "Give me a D" (children shout "D" and wave their pompons). "Give me another D" (children shout "D" and wave their pompons). "What does that spell?" (children shout, "Todd. Yea, Todd" and wave their pompons).

Ask an outgoing child to lead his or her own cheer first. Usually all children like doing this, but if you think a child might find it embarrassing to lead the cheer, you can lead it for him or her.

Class Handshake

Have the children in your class develop a unique handshake greeting, such as slap your own knees, clap your friend's hands, grab your friend's right wrist, grab your friend's left wrist and shake three times. Have them use it as a friendship greeting whenever they meet.

Make sure the class doesn't exclude those who don't know the handshake. Have your class teach the handshake to each new class member to make him or her feel special and welcome.

68

Peer Interviews 2-5

Make enough photocopies of the question list at the left so there's one list for every two children. Have children form pairs. Give the children two or three minutes to ask their partners one of the questions from the list. When the time is up, form a circle. Have children each share what they learned about their partner.

Questions:

1. If you could be any animal, what would you be? Why?

2. If you could be invisible for an hour, what would you do?

3. If you could be any person in the Bible, who would you be? Why?

4. If you had the chance to sit next to Jesus and ask one question, what would you ask?

5. What do you like to do most when you're all by yourself?

Practicing Love

Set up a quiet corner with a small table, a chair and a tape recorder. Write down each child's name on a slip of paper and put the slips in a can. Have each child draw a name from the can.

Go on with class as usual, but, one at a time, let children sit in the corner and tape-record an affirming message for the person they drew from the can. For example, Billy might tape-record this message: "This is Billy. I think David reads very well." Have an adult or teenage assistant available to help children work the tape recorder and to ensure that the messages are all positive.

Toward the end of the class session, play the recording back to the children.

Listen

Have children pick partners they don't know very well. Have pairs find out three things about each other they didn't know before.

Say: **Be sure to listen carefully to your partner. When we listen carefully, we show people that we care about them and what they have to say.**

Give the children three minutes to exchange information. Then bring the class members back together and have them sit in a circle.

Go around the circle and have children each share what they learned about their partner.

When all have shared, have the partners thank each other for listening carefully.

Silver-Boxed Boost

Here's a great way to wrap up a compliment. If you have fewer than 12 students, wrap one small box in silver paper and put a silver bow on top. If you have more than 12 students, divide the children into groups with six to 12 students and provide a wrapped silver box for each group.

Tell the children that giving a compliment is like giving someone a beautiful box full of encouragement.

Give the box to one of the children and compliment him or her. For example, say, "You're a real leader in our class." If you have more than one group of children, give the box to one child and have the class members watch so they know what to do. Then have the groups continue on their own.

The child who receives the silver box presents it to another child within the group and offers words of encouragement.

Continue until every child has received a compliment. No one should receive the silver box more than once.

Talent Scouts

Find out the special talents and interests of each child in your class. Then schedule a time during the year for the class to see each child involved in his or her special activity.

You might go to a band performance, a play or a speech contest. You might go to look at artwork or a 4-H Club display. Maybe some children would like to demonstrate a skill, such as baking cookies or showing the tricks that he or she has taught a pet.

Being "talent scouts" helps the class appreciate the unique talents of each class member.

If your class is too large to make traveling to each event practical, have each child give a presentation about his or her special interest.

You're Beary Nice

Try this activity to encourage children to notice positive traits in others. Photocopy enough bears from the next page so every child has one bear for each classmate.

First, have children write their classmates' names on the bears, one name per bear. Make sure they each make a bear for themselves. Then have children write a positive characteristic on each child's bear, such as "You're always kind to others."

When all the bears have been completed, have children deliver their bear messages to the other children. Then have children connect their bears' paws together with glue or paper fasteners to make garlands. Mount the garlands on a bulletin board with a sign that reads, "Beary Kind Boys and Girls." After a couple of weeks, send the garlands home.

72

Love Notes

This is a great project for the month of February when you're talking about love. Tell children that Paul wrote letters to various churches and encouraged them with love messages. Use Bible passages such as Ephesians 6:23-24; Philippians 1:3-4, 6; and Philippians 4:1.

Give children each a lunch bag; then have them decorate it with markers and put their name on it. Hang the lunch bags around the room with tape or tacks.

Distribute red and pink construction paper and scissors. Have children cut out a heart for each of their classmates. Tell children to write a special love note of encouragement on each child's heart. Have children place each note in the appropriate bag.

When the children leave, have them take their notes home to read. Next week, ask how the notes made them feel.

Ask:
● **How many times did you read the notes during the week?**
● **Did the notes change your attitude about yourself?**
● **How do you feel toward the people who wrote to you?**

It's All in Your Name

Give each student a 3×5 card and a pencil. Have children each write their first name vertically along the left edge of the card, one letter per line. Collect the cards, mix them up and redistribute them, one card per person. Be sure no one gets his or her own card.

Have students think of words or phrases that describe the person whose name they've drawn, and write each one on the card. The words or phrases should begin with the letters of the name. For example, someone who draws Seth's card might write:

<u>S</u>illy and lots of fun to be with

<u>E</u>nergetic

<u>T</u>ries his best all the time

<u>H</u>elps others

Be sure to help children with spelling.

Have the children read the cards aloud, and then hand them back to their owners.

Building Bricks

2-6

U se this activity to show children what it means to build one another up. You'll need bricks and permanent markers or paint pens. Paving bricks work best because they have the smoothest surface.

Give each child a brick. Have them each write their name on their brick with a permanent marker or a paint pen.

Form groups of no more than six children. Have each group sit in a circle and tell the children to each pass their brick one person to the right. Have the children write one or two encouraging words on the bricks they received. Have the children continue passing the bricks and writing messages on them until the bricks are returned to their owners.

Then have the children build a pyramid with their bricks. Read 1 Thessalonians 5:11: "So encourage each other to build each other up, just as you are already doing" (Living Bible).

Thank the children for building one another up, just as bricks build a building.

Kindness Gifts

2-6

Give children each a pencil and two slips of paper. On one slip, have them each write down some act of kindness they can do for a classmate during class, such as getting a glass of water, giving a back rub or telling a joke. Put all these slips into a can. On the other slip, have them each write their name. Put all these slips into another can.

Read Mark 10:43-44. Then say: **Let's take turns practicing our greatness.** Have children each draw an act of kindness from one can and a student's name from the other can. Have each child read the slips aloud and do the act of kindness for the other student.

When all the children have given and received a kindness, say: **It may have felt great to have someone serve you, but true greatness comes in serving one another. When you serve one another, you're showing others they're special.**

Secret Admirers

2-6

Have each child write his or her name and address on the back of a stamped postcard. Shuffle the postcards and then pass them out. Make sure no one gets his or her own postcard. Have children each write their secret pal a complimentary note. For example, someone may write, "I think you're a really good baseball player." Tell the children not to sign their names!

Mail the postcards the next day. Read all the cards before mailing them to catch any negative messages. If there are any, write that child a positive message yourself.

The following week, let the children each guess who their secret admirer is. This should provide lots of laughs and good fun.

"Guess Who" Surveys

Make enough photocopies of the survey for everyone in your class. Have the children fill out the surveys and secretly turn them in. Next time you meet, announce to the children that you've selected a person to be the Mystery Person for the Day.

Using the survey sheets, give hints about the Mystery Person's identity, such as "This person loves the color blue and has five people living in his or her home along with FiFi and Snake Breath. This person hopes to travel in a rocket to Mars." When children guess the Mystery Person's identity, let that child wear a construction paper star that says, "I'm special!"

Choose a different child every week until all the children have been the Mystery Person for the Day.

Survey

1. Your name: _____

2. Your favorite color:_____

3. Your favorite food: _____

4. Your hobbies: _____

5. Your favorite TV show: _____

6. The names of the animals that live in your home:
_____

7. Your dream vacation:_____

8. Your favorite subject in school: _____

9. Your favorite song:_____

10. The number of people living in your home: _____

Chains of Friendship

2-6

Give each child a small box or manila envelope. Make a bunch of 1×6-inch paper slips. You'll need at least enough slips to make a paper chain that'll encircle your room.

Each time your class meets, have students fill out several paper slips with statements they made or actions they did that encouraged friends or family members. Have the kids put their slips in their boxes or envelopes.

Every few weeks, have the kids make links out of the paper slips in their boxes and hook the links together to make a paper chain. Have children hook their paper chains together to make one large paper chain. Then hang the paper chain in your classroom.

This can be a never-ending activity. Have the children continue adding to the paper chain all year until it circles your classroom several times. At the end of the year, send a segment of the chain home with each child and have him or her hang it up at home as a reminder to encourage friends and family.

For even more fun, continue until the paper chain will encircle your church's sanctuary. With your pastor's permission, declare one worship time as Friendship Encouragement Day. Hang the paper chain in the sanctuary and put a paragraph in the bulletin that explains your class's project to the rest of the church. Invite each member of the congregation to take home a link as a reminder to encourage friends and family.

Special Notes Board

2-6

Designate a bulletin board in your room as the Special Notes Board. This is a place where children can leave affirming notes for one another. Provide markers and construction paper shapes, such as hearts and stars, near the board for them to write on. Use seasonal shapes, too, such as colored leaves for fall, angels for Christmas, snowflakes for winter and suns for summer.

Provide a couple of minutes before and after class for children to write their notes. Encourage children to affirm one another for things that describe their character rather than the outward appearance. For example, notes such as "Krista is fun to play with because she's always a good sport" or "Krista is a peacemaker" mean much more than "Krista has pretty new shoes."

Read the notes to find out if someone is left out. You could secretly ask a child to watch a forgotten child during the class and write two positive notes about the child by the end of the class.

At the end of each week or month, clean off the board and let the children take home the notes written about them.

Write and Rub

3-5

Before the children arrive, write several affirmations on slips of paper. Keep the affirmations simple, no more than three words long. For example, you could write, "You're God's child," "I like you," "God loves you" and "You are special." Put the slips of paper in a can or a basket.

Have children form pairs and sit cross-legged on the floor. Have one child from each pair draw out a slip of paper, read it to him- or herself and put the slip back in the can. Then that child uses a finger to write the message on his or her partner's back. The partner guesses what is being written.

When the person guesses what has been written on his or her back, the partners switch places and play again.

Juicy Fruit

Put a good taste in the mouths and hearts of your class members by getting them to identify the fruit of the Spirit in one another.

Before class, copy the "Juicy Fruit of the Spirit" diagram on a sheet of newsprint or posterboard.

When class begins, pass out sticks of Juicy Fruit gum to get a good taste in everyone's mouth! Then have everyone write his or her name on a slip of paper and put it in a bowl.

Next, have each person do the following, one person at a time:

● Pick a name from the bowl.

● Go to the "Juicy Fruit of the Spirit" poster and sign that person's name next to the fruit of the Spirit that best matches him or her.

● Explain why that fruit was chosen.

After everyone has taken a turn, look at the poster and discuss the class's strengths and potential growth areas. Pray a prayer of thanksgiving, thanking God for the gifts he's given each member of your class.

Juicy Fruit of the Spirit

Love	Joy	Peace
Patience	Kindness	Goodness
Faithfulness	Gentleness	Self-Control

Pinky Links

Have children choose partners. Tell children to each think of five things they like about their partner. Explain that when a person says something about his or her partner, he or she holds up a pinky finger. The person's partner replies, "Thank you" and links pinky fingers with the person. The praise-giving partner says a second thing about his or her partner, the partner says, "Thank you" and they link ring fingers. Have them continue until all five fingers are linked together.

Then have them switch roles and do the activity again. Afterward, say: **Just as your finger links became stronger with each praise you shared, our friendships with our Christian brothers and sisters become stronger when we praise one another.**

Heavy Burdens

For each child, you'll need a medium-sized rock and a perma-nent marker. Read Galatians 6:2. Have the children write something that is bothering them on their rocks. Have chil-dren stand in a line on the side of the room across from the door.

Then have the children form pairs. In each pair, have one per-son say, "I'll carry your burden to fulfill Christ's law," pray one sen-tence to ask God's help in relieving the partner's problem, pick up the partner's rock and carry it outside the door. Then have the other person do the same for his or her partner.

Ask:

● **How does it feel to know your partner will help you with your burden?**

● **Why is it important for us to carry each other's bur-dens?**

Say: **The way we treat other people shows what we think**

of them. God created each of us to be special members of his family. When we help others with their troubles, we show them how important they are.

Fire Power

Rekindle the "fire" in your class by blessing one another in a candle-lighting activity. Have the class form a circle. Pass out unlit candles to each child.

Light a candle and turn out the classroom lights. Rejoin the circle and turn to the child next to you. Light his or her candle and complete this sentence: "I'm glad Jesus makes his light shine through you because ..."

That child turns to the next child, lights his or her candle and completes the sentence. Continue until everyone's candle is lit.

Say: **This room was dark. But because of Jesus' light shining so brightly in each of you, this room is full of beautiful light.**

Building Esteem
From
Child to Others

Praise Him, Praise Him

Preschool-K

Sing the old favorite "Praise Him, Praise Him, All Ye Little Children" but add verses that'll teach children to recognize the efforts of other people. Try these verses:

Praise Mom	Praise brothers
Praise Dad	Praise friends
Praise sisters	Praise teachers

After each verse, ask the children what they could praise those people for. Encourage children to think of other people they can praise and make up new verses for them.

After singing all the verses children can think of, have children each choose someone to praise this week. Then have each child decide what he or she will do to praise that person.

Pray: **Dear God, thank you for giving us so many people in our lives to praise. Help us to praise someone this week.**

Thumb Books

Preschool-2

Send a book of greetings to someone who could use some cheer.

Give each child a 3×5 card. Have children each press their thumb on a stamp pad and make a thumbprint on their card.

Then have children each add features to their thumbprint to make it look like a person or an animal. Look at the example for ideas. Have children each sign their name to their card.

Collect the cards into a deck, put a blank card on top and staple the left edges together. On the top card write a message such as "Thumbody wants you to get well soon" or "Thumbody says thank you for teaching the kindergarten class last week."

Prayer Grams

Preschool–6

Photocopy the "prayer gram" below. Have children choose people in the church to pray for. Set aside a few minutes in class for children to pray for them. With younger children, it works best to choose one person and pray for him or her as a class. Older children can pray independently.

Then have children fill out prayer grams for the people they prayed for. Younger children will need help with spelling. If you're working with preschoolers, fill out the prayer gram yourself and have the children color it.

Have the children address envelopes and put the prayer grams inside. You can get addresses for many church members from the church office. Mail the prayer grams on your way home from church.

Prayer Gram

Dear _____,

_____ prayed for you today. May God give you many special blessings.

Helping Hands

U se this activity to help young children appreciate those around them.
Ask:

● **What can hands do to help people?**

Encourage all kinds of responses from clapping for a performance to giving back rubs to washing the dishes. Have children act out their responses.

Ask:

● **Has anyone ever used his or her hands to help you? What did that person do for you?**

Say: **Let's thank those people for using their hands to help us.**

Give each child a sheet of paper on which you've written the words, "Helping Hands Award" at the top. At the bottom of each sheet, write, "Thank you for helping me _____."
Help children fill in the blank with the answer to the last question. Older children can write the words themselves.

Fill shallow pans with tempera paint in different colors. Have children dip their hands in the paint and press them onto their papers. Have cleanup supplies handy to keep paint from being spread all over the room.

Set the awards aside to dry. When they're dry, encourage the children to present them to their helpers.

Get Well Soon

G ive each child a square of lipstick blotting paper or eyeglass cleaning paper. Have the children each use a Q-Tip or a small brush to put on lipstick and kiss their paper. Encourage hesitant children to just draw lips. Have washcloths and soap available so children can wash the lipstick off their mouths.

Glue the squares of paper to a card or banner, and add the words, "Just thought we'd kiss it and make it better." Add 2 Corinthians 13:12, "Greet each other with a holy kiss."

Send this get well greeting to a sick friend.

Hug Club

Get your class to start a Hug Club. Choose one or more of these ideas to teach your class members how to love one another.

● Establish a membership requirement that each member must give a minimum of six hugs per day.

● Put up posters that say, "Hug Crossings" in your church. Those who cross paths by the poster have to hug.

● Hand out coupons for free hugs.

● Create a weekly "hugger's hit list" of specific people club members will make sure they hug.

● Raise funds by starting a Hugs Delivery Service. This works like a singing telegram service. Church members hire your class to hug specific individuals. Deliver hugs as a class. You could charge a dollar a hug, or you could even do it as a service project to spread joy through your congregation.

● Host a Hug Party. Celebrate the different types of hugs at this party, such as bearhugs, one-to-one hugs, pinky finger hugs and group hugs—have your children come up with all kinds of zany hugs. Serve Teddy Grahams to represent bearhugs or make fruit hugs by wrapping Fruit Roll-ups around cheese strips.

Chalk It Up

Spread colorful tidings of good news with this easy esteem-builder. Have your class choose someone to recognize, such as a parent, the pastor, the custodian or the church bus driver.

Use colored chalk to decorate a thank you card on your church's parking lot, on the sidewalk that leads from the sanctuary to the parking lot or even on the driveway of your honoree's house.

Even though the chalk will wash off easily in the next good rain, it's a good idea to get permission from someone in the church office or from a family member before you begin this activity.

To save time, quickly write the message of praise or thanks with colored chalk yourself. For example, to thank the bus driver you could write, "Thank you, Mr. Gooding, for driving our bus." Then have the children decorate the words, add drawings and sign their names.

This is also a great way to publicly thank people in the community, such as a business that donated supplies for vacation Bible school.

Smiles Are Catching

Have children take turns being greeters for church. Tell them to greet each person with a big smile and say, "Good morning." Say: **Watch what happens when you greet people. Count how many smiles you get in return for your smile.**

With younger children you may want to make necklaces or nametags for them that say, "I'm a greeter" so adults will realize what they're doing.

Try this easy-to-make necklace. On a sheet of construction paper, write, "My name is_____. I'm a greeter." Have children each write their name on the line and decorate their paper. Punch a hole in the top of each paper and thread a piece of yarn through the hole.

Tie the yarn around the child's neck.

It's also a good idea to have a teenage or adult helper stand with younger children.

Afterward, ask the children how many people smiled back at them. Say: **Today, each of you did a great job spreading God's joy to the people you greeted. Thank you for making them feel important and welcome at our church.**

Secret Person of the Month K-6

Prepare a list of people your class wants to show appreciation for. This list could include pastors, teachers, custodians, worship leaders, former teachers or youth leaders, babysitters, shut-ins or kitchen workers.

Each month, select one person from the list to be the secret person of the month—only the children in the class know about the project. During the month, children in the class should make the selected person feel special and appreciated.

Here are some ideas to make the person of the month feel special:

- draw pictures,
- make "thinking of you" greeting cards,
- bake a treat,
- give a bearhug,
- shake his or her hand,
- send postcards or
- wash his or her car windows during church.

Choose several things to do as a class and as individuals. Ask children for their ideas on how to make each person of the month feel appreciated.

Flowers Say It Best

When your class wants to thank someone, have the children make and send a tissue bouquet! For each flower, you'll need two facial tissues. Fold each tissue accordion style. Put one folded tissue on top of the other and fold them in half. Hold the folded end and twist it so the four "petals" are evenly distributed. Tape the twisted end. Then separate the tissue layers to make eight petals. The blossom should look similar to a carnation.

Wrap the bottom with green floral tape. Add construction paper leaves and make stems out of green floral wire. Secure them to the blossom with more floral tape. Add a dab of floral-scented perfume, such as jasmine, lilac or honeysuckle, to the center of the blossom.

Put the flowers in a vase, or wrap them in tissue paper and put them in a long florists box. Be sure to enclose a card signed by each class member.

People Who Serve God

Ask each child to think of a person in the church and act out what he or she does to serve God. Have the rest of the children guess who the person is. For example, children could act out the roles of janitor, teacher, nursery attendant or usher.

When the children have guessed who each person is, have them each write a thank you note to the person they portrayed.

Or, set up a video camera and videotape this game of Charades. Set up a television in the church lobby before or after a church service so people can view the video. The adults will be touched when they see the children have noticed them serving God.

We're Nuts About You

3-6

Give each child a small piece of tan construction paper. Have children draw and cut out peanut shapes. Photocopy the pattern for children to trace. Give the children black markers so they can write their names on the peanuts and add marks to make the peanuts look realistic. Provide a few real peanuts for children to munch on while they work.

Put all the paper peanuts in an

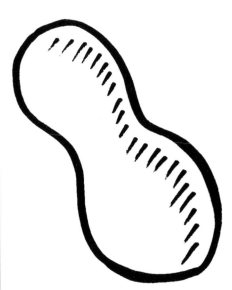

empty peanut jar. Add a card that says, "We're Nuts About You!"
Inside the card, write a message of thanks. For example, "Thank
you, Mrs. Smiley! The third-grade class of First Church thanks
you for leading our praise and worship time during the summer.
We learned a lot of fun songs and had a great time. You helped us
praise God in a new way."

All Puffed Up

4-6

H ave children sit in a circle. Show them an uninflated balloon.
Say: **This balloon represents kids in fourth to sixth
grade. Let's see what happens when kids start bragging about themselves.**

Go around the circle and have children each share something that
children their age say when they brag about themselves. Kids might
say things like, "My clothes are better than anyone else's" or "Of
course I got the best grade, I'm smarter than anyone else I know."
For each thing they mention, breathe some air into the balloon.

By the time everyone has shared something, the balloon
should be so full of air that it's about to pop. Continue adding air
until it does pop, or you can just pop it with a pin if you don't want
it to explode in your face.

Read 1 Corinthians 8:1.

Ask:

● **Why is bragging about yourself not a good idea?**
● **What kind of attitude should you have about yourself?**

Read Galatians 6:3-5.

Say: **We know God thinks we're important because he
created us and sent his son to die for us. Each of us is special, and we should be proud of who we are. But God
doesn't mean for us to consider ourselves better than others. Instead of bragging about how much better we are than
others, we can love ourselves as part of God's creation and
build each other up in love.**

Form groups of five and give each group a pack of bubble gum
with five pieces of gum. In each group, have each child take a piece

of bubble gum and finish this sentence: "Instead of puffing myself up, I'll build up my friends in love by..." Kids might finish the sentence with "saying 'Great job!' when they beat me in a race" or "being happy for them when good things happen to them."

Bible Lessons Your Kids Will Remember...

6-Minute Messages for Children

Donald Hinchey

Here's the perfect resource for the busy children's worker who wants to give an excellent children's devotion without all the work. Now it's easy to deliver meaningful children's messages that kids enjoy and remember. Instead of a simple object-lesson lecture ...

- each message uses a concrete experience,
- kids are encouraged to share their feelings,
- many lessons include a skit or game, and
- some messages suggest simple take-home memory aids.

Each message is based on an important Christian theme and Bible text with a helpful list of needed supplies. Great for Sunday school opening exercises, children's church, midweek meetings ... any time you need a quick children's devotion.

ISBN 1-55945-170-X $9.99

Amazing Stories From Genesis

13 Easy-to-Use Lessons for Grades 3–4

Cindy Smith

Here's everything you need for quick planning and faith-building fun. Your third- and fourth-grade kids will discover that ...

- God is here and with us now
- God creates us to care
- God gives us choices and forgives us when we fail
- God hears us when we hurt and protects us

You'll introduce your kids to the first people of the Bible ... Adam and Eve, Cain and Abel, Noah, Abraham, and more. Each lesson gives you ...

- easy-to-follow instructions
- Bible storytelling that actively involves kids
- art activities that help bring the stories to life for kids
- get-up-and-go games to grab and hold kids' attention

... plus many lessons contain reproducible handouts.

Amazing Stories from Genesis will bring the Bible to life in your classroom and challenge your students to learn more about our amazing God.

ISBN 1-55945-094-0 $12.99

More Practical Resources for Your Ministry to Children...

Children's Ministry Care Cards™

Inspire and affirm your kids. Each card has a fun cartoon to capture children's interest—and an easy-to-understand Bible verse to teach young people about God.

Affirmations
Uplifting messages to brighten a child's day and encourage his or her faith.
ISBN 1-55945-181-5

Birthday Greetings
Make your kids feel special—and boost their self-esteem.
ISBN 1-55945-182-3

Each tear-off booklet of 30 full-color postcards contains 6 different messages for only $6.99.

Lively Bible Lessons

You can make creative teaching a snap with these 20 complete children's Bible lessons for each age level. Lively is better, because kids learn more. Each lesson has at least six child-size activities including easy-to-do crafts, action songs, attention-grabbing games, and snacks that reinforce the message. Plus, innovative new lessons are included to celebrate holidays like Valentine's Day, Easter, Thanksgiving, and Christmas. Just read the simple instructions, gather a few easy-to-find supplies, and you're ready to go!

Preschoolers
ISBN 1-55945-067-3, $10.99

Kindergarten
ISBN 1-55945-097-5, $10.99

Grades K–3
ISBN 1-55945-074-6, $10.99

Grades 1–2
ISBN 1-55945-098-3, $10.99

Recharge Your Ministry With Fresh Ideas...

Making Scripture Stick

Lisa Flinn & Barbara Younger

Discover 52 unforgettable Bible verse adventures for children in grades 1–5. You'll use creative, hands-on learning techniques that draw kids into a world of imagination, discovery, and creative interaction. Bible verses come alive with these active, fun adventures as kids...

- make paper tambourines and use them to create a new song of praise (Psalm 150:4).
- run finger races and discuss the challenges that Christians face (Hebrews 12:1).
- blow bubbles and see that bubbles last an instant while God's love is forever (Psalm 90:2).
- make a foot-paint footprint banner and see how God watches their every step (Job 31:4).

The easy-to-prepare lessons feature a simple format, clear directions, inexpensive materials, reproducible handouts, and a wide variety of exciting activities. And follow-up discussions make the Bible messages stick!

ISBN 1–55945–093-2 $10.99

Quick Games for Children's Ministry

Discover 100 active, creative games for kids from preschool through sixth grade. More than just filling time, you'll use these games to...

- increase Bible knowledge,
- teach teamwork,
- reinforce your lesson,
- build group unity, and
- have fun!

Each game has been field-tested by children's workers from across the country. Plus, you'll appreciate how quick and easy these games are to prepare—with few or no supplies needed! Perfect for use in Sunday school, vacation Bible school, children's church, summer camp—wherever you have a group of kids.

ISBN 1-55945-157-2 $9.99